Cambridge Young Learners English Tests

Cambridge Starters 7

Examination papers from

University of Cambridge ESOL Examinations:

English for Speakers of Other Languages

CAMBRIDGE
UNIVERSITY PRESS

CAMBRIDGE UNIVERSITY PRESS
Cambridge, New York, Melbourne, Madrid, Cape Town,
Singapore, São Paulo, Delhi, Mexico City

Cambridge University Press
The Edinburgh Building, Cambridge CB2 8RU, UK

www.cambridge.org
Information on this title: www.cambridge.org/9780521173674

First published 2011
4th printing 2013

Printed in Dubai by Oriental Press

A catalogue record for this publication is available from the British Library

ISBN 978-0-521-17367-4 Student's Book
ISBN 978-0-521-17369-8 Answer Booklet
ISBN 978-0-521-17370-4 Audio CD

Cover design by David Lawton
Produced by Peter & Jan Simmonett

Contents

Part 1
– 5 questions –

Listen and draw lines. There is one example.

Part 2
– 5 questions –

Read the question. Listen and write a name or a number.

There are two examples.

Examples

What's the girl's name? .... Kim ....

How many brothers has she got? .... 1 ....

Questions

1   What's Kim's brother's name?   ....

2   How old is Kim's brother?   ....

3   What's Kim's family name?   ....

4   What's the name of Kim's school?   .... Street School

5   What number is Kim's flat?   ....

Part 3
– 5 questions –

Listen and tick (✔) the box. There is one example.

What's Mum cleaning?

A ☐   B ✔   C ☐

1   What are Anna's favourite animals in the zoo?

A ☐   B ☐   C ☐

2   What's in Bill's lunch box?

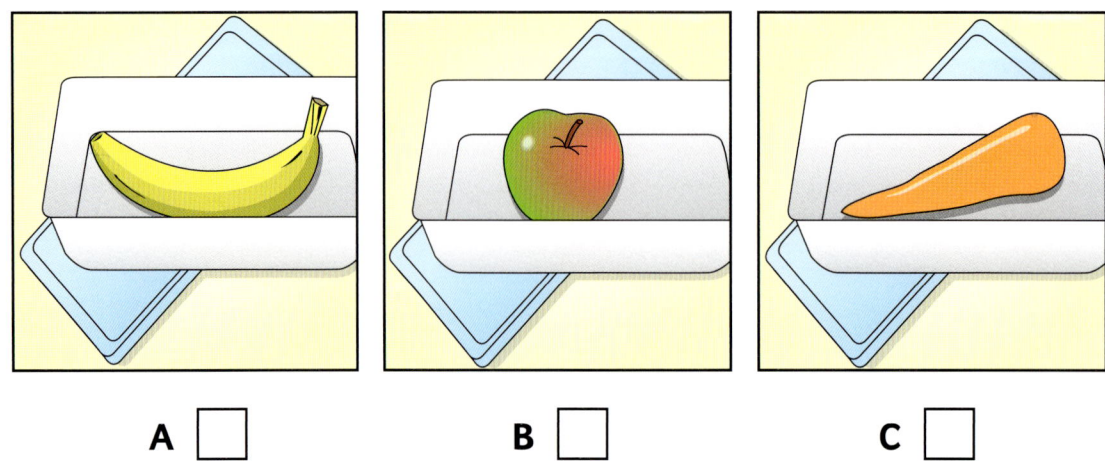

A ☐   B ☐   C ☐

3   Which sport does Tony play at school?

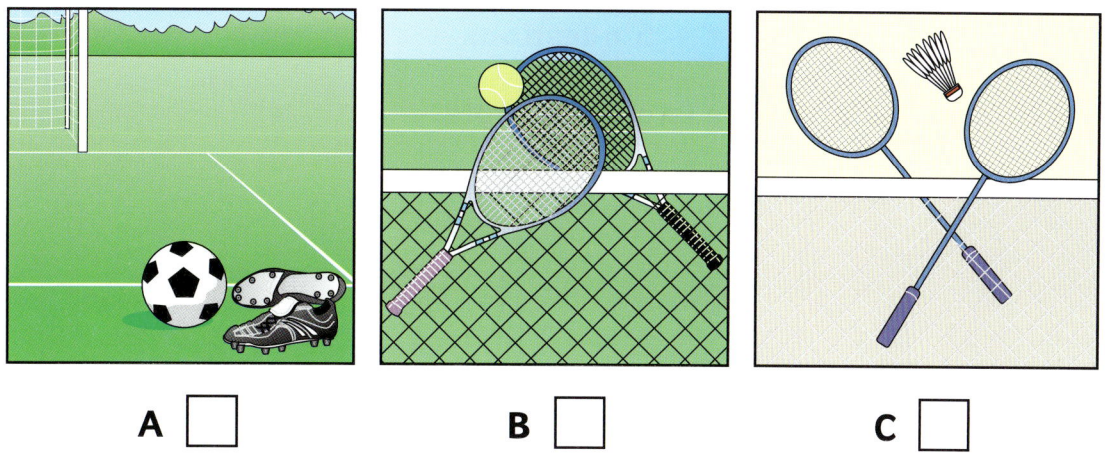

A ☐   B ☐   C ☐

4   Where's Grandpa?

A ☐   B ☐   C ☐

5   What would Nick like to do?

A ☐   B ☐   C ☐

Part 4

– 5 questions –

Listen and colour. There is one example.

Reading and Writing

Part 1

– 5 questions –

Look and read. Put a tick (✔) or a cross (✗) in the box.
There are two examples.

Examples

This is a face.

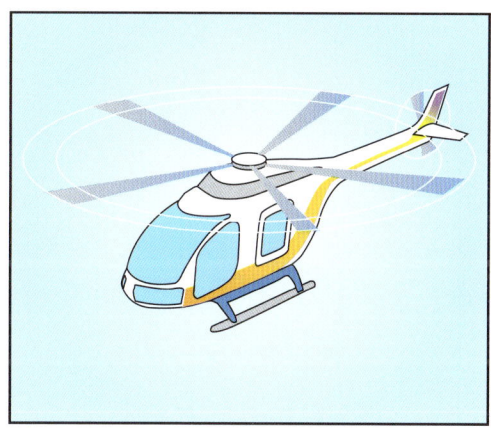

This is a plane.

Questions

1

This is a potato.

2

This is a snake. ☐

3

This is a jacket. ☐

4

This is an eraser. ☐

5

This is a cupboard. ☐

Part 2

– 5 questions –

Look and read. Write yes or no.

Examples

The woman is wearing a brown skirt.	yes
The baby is sleeping.	no

Questions

1   There is a dog in front of the door. ....

2   There are some pears on the tree. ....

3   The girl is giving food to the ducks. ....

4   There is a goat behind the flowers. ....

5   The old man is standing up. ....

Part 3

– 5 questions –

Look at the pictures. Look at the letters. Write the words.

Example

<u>k</u> <u>i</u> <u>t</u> <u>e</u>

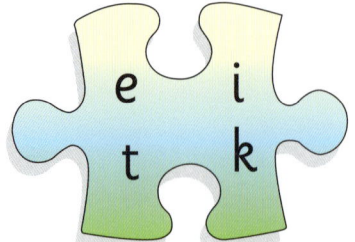

Questions

1

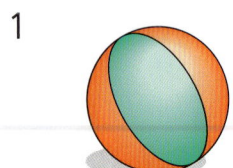

_ _ _ _

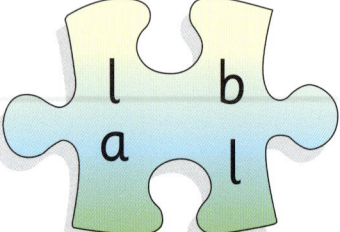

2

_ _ _ _

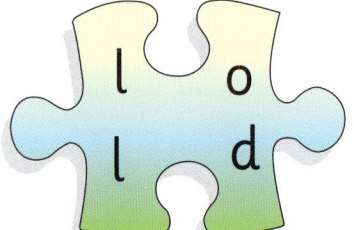

3

_ _ _ _ _

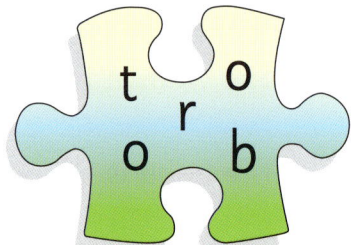

4

_ _ _ _ _

5

_ _ _ _ _ _

Part 4

– 5 questions –

Read this. Choose a word from the box. Write the correct word next to numbers 1–5. There is one example.

A desk

I am next to the ....window........ in Ben's bedroom. Ben is a

young (**1**)........................... . He sits on a (**2**)...........................

next to me. He paints pictures on me and he reads

(**3**)........................... . There is a new (**4**)...........................

on me too and Ben writes stories and he plays

(**5**)........................... on it.

What am I? I'm a desk.

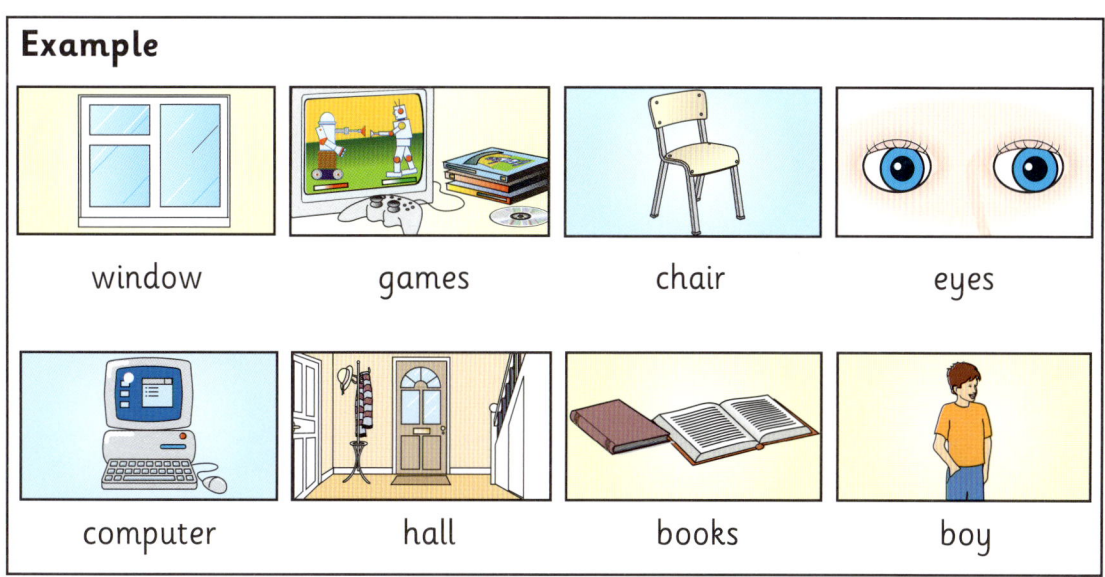

Example			
window	games	chair	eyes
computer	hall	books	boy

Part 5

– 5 questions –

Look at the pictures and read the questions. Write one-word answers.

Examples

What is the woman cleaning? the ....floor.......

What colour is the wall? ....green.......

Questions

1 Which room is she in? the ....

2   What has the girl got in her hand?   a ....

3   Who has got dirty shoes?   the two ....

4   Where is the phone now?   on the ....

5   Who looks happy?   the ....

Blank Page

Listening

Part 1

– 5 questions –

Listen and draw lines. There is one example.

Part 2
– 5 questions –

Read the question. Listen and write a name or a number.

There are two examples.

Examples

What's the boy's name? .... *Alex*

How old is he? 9

Questions

1   What's the name of Alex's friend?   ....

2   Where does she live?   .... Street

3   What's the number of her house?   ....

4   How old is she?   ....

5   What's the name of her dog?   ....

Part 3
– 5 questions –

Listen and tick (✔) the box. There is one example.

What's May drinking?

A ☐   B ✔   C ☐

1   What's Ben's favourite animal?

A ☐   B ☐   C ☐

2   What is Anna drawing?

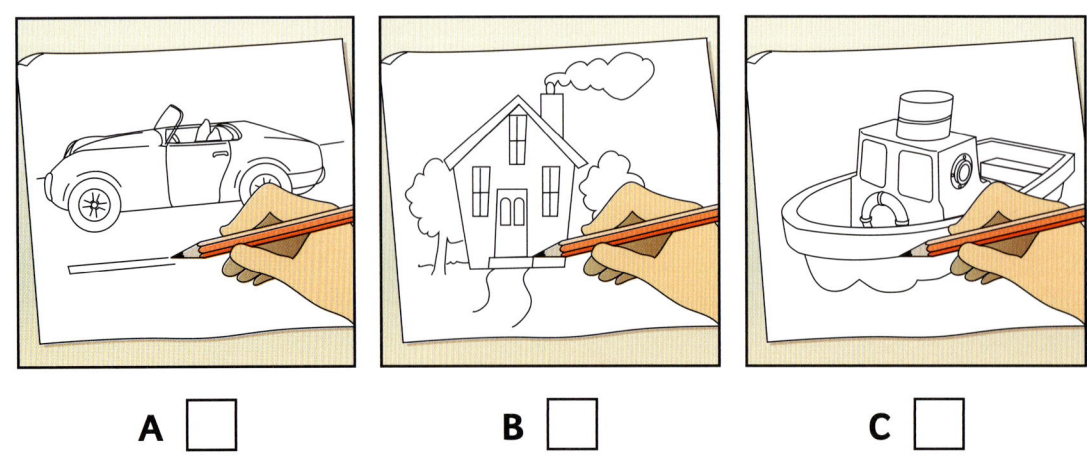

A ☐   B ☐   C ☐

3   Where's Nick's mouse?

A ☐   B ☐   C ☐

4   What's Grandfather doing now?

A ☐   B ☐   C ☐

5   Which is Sam's picture?

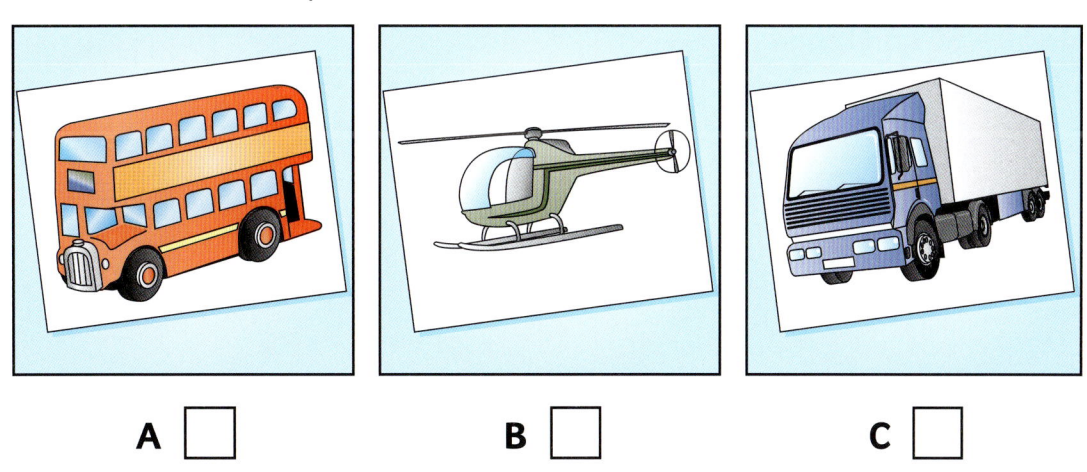

A ☐   B ☐   C ☐

Part 4

– 5 questions –

Listen and colour. There is one example.

Reading and Writing

Part 1
– 5 questions –

**Look and read. Put a tick (✔) or a cross (✗) in the box.
There are two examples.**

Examples

This is a skirt.

This is a horse.

Questions

1

This is a plane.

2

This is a potato. ☐

3

This is a piano. ☐

4

This is a sausage. ☐

5

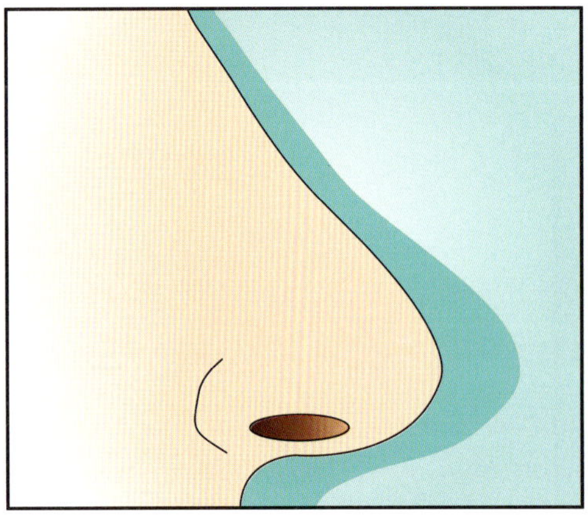

This is an ear. ☐

Part 2

– 5 questions –

Look and read. Write yes or no.

Examples

The man has got a boat.   *yes*

Some children are playing football.   *no*

Questions

1   There is a cat on the wall.   ....

2   The monsters are wearing shoes.   ....

3   The boy has got a kite.   ....

4   The girl is waving at the monsters.   ....

5   There are five ducks in the water.   ....

Part 3
– 5 questions –

Look at the pictures. Look at the letters. Write the words.

Example

<u>d</u> <u>o</u> <u>l</u> <u>l</u>

Questions

1

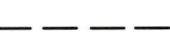

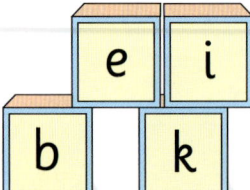

2

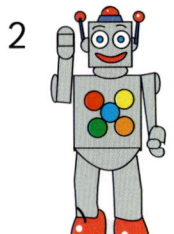

_ _ _ _ _

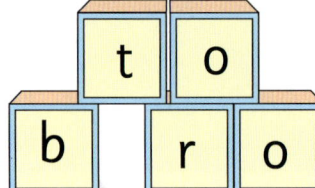

3

_ _ _ _ _

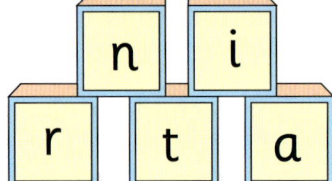

4

_ _ _ _ _ _

5

_ _ _ _ _ _ _ _

Part 4
– 5 questions –

Read this. Choose a word from the box. Write the correct word next to numbers 1–5. There is one example.

A garden

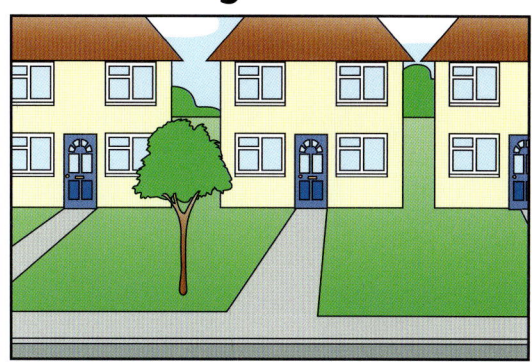

I am between the .... *street* .... and a house.

A (**1**).................... lives in the house. The children play

(**2**).................... and tennis in me. The father sits on a

(**3**).................... and reads in me.

There is a tree. Some (**4**).................... live in it.

The children eat big, red (**5**).................... from one tree.

What am I? I am a garden.

Example			
street	apples	birds	family
badminton	computer	chair	camera

Part 5
– 5 questions –

Look at the pictures and read the questions. Write one-word answers.

Examples

Where is the man?   in the   bedroom
....

What is he doing?   sleeping
....

Questions

1   Where are the man's glasses?   under the   ....

30

2   Which room is the phone in?   the ....

3   Who is opening the door?   the ....

4   What has the man got in his hand?   a ....

5   Where are the girl and the boy?   on the ....

Blank Page

Listening

Part 1
– 5 questions –

Listen and draw lines. There is one example.

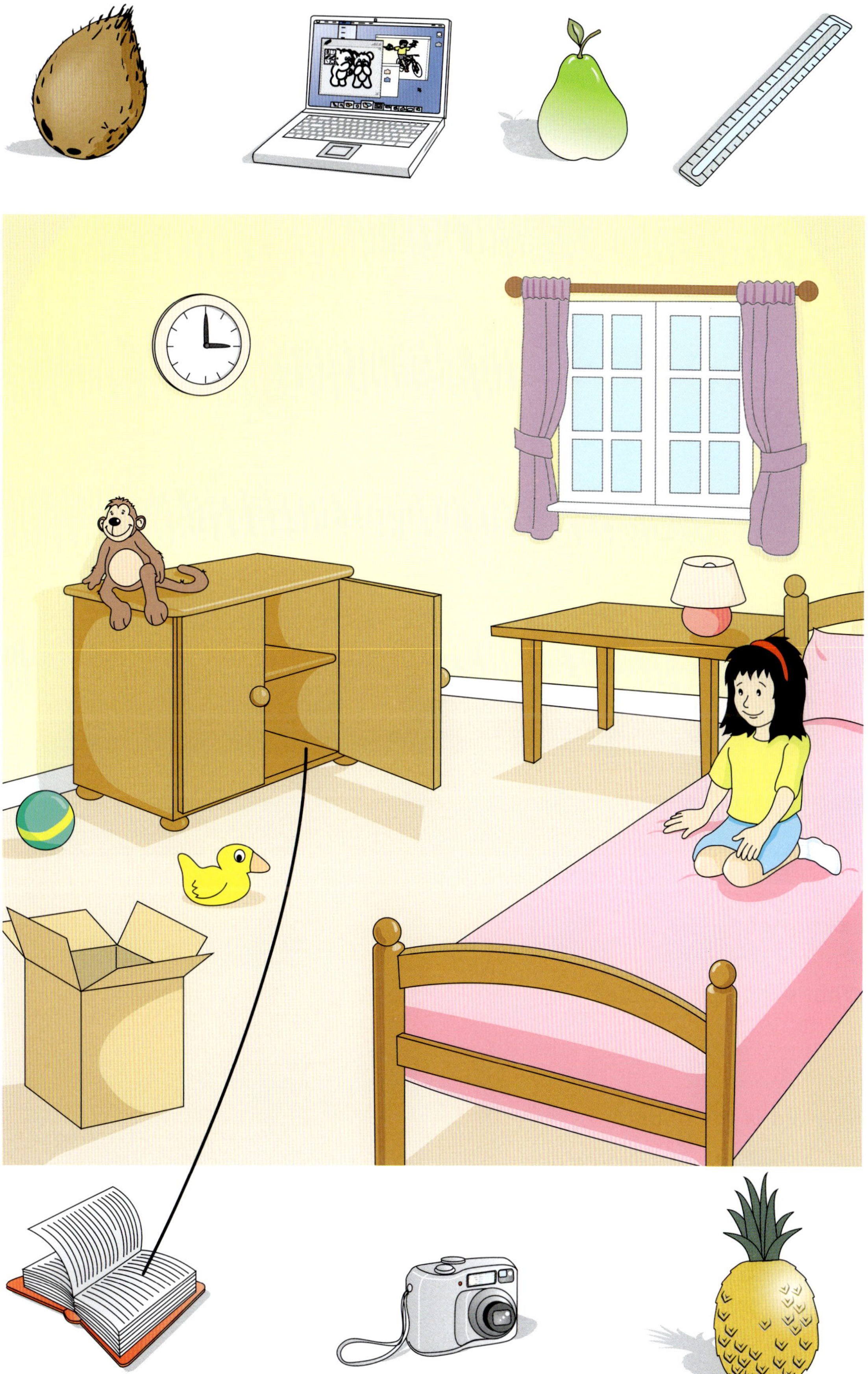

Part 2
– 5 questions –

Read the question. Listen and write a name or a number.

There are two examples.

Examples

What's the boy's name?   Tony
....

How old is the boy?   11
....

Questions

1   How many sisters has Tony got?   ....

2   What's the name of Tony's
    favourite sister?   ....

3   Where does Tony's family live?   .... Street

4   What's the number of Tony's house?   ....

5   What's the name of Tony's friend?   ....

Part 3
– 5 questions –

Listen and tick (✔) the box. There is one example.

What's May giving Ben for his birthday?

A ✔   B ☐   C ☐

1   Where's the soccer game?

A ☐   B ☐   C ☐

2   What's Bill doing?

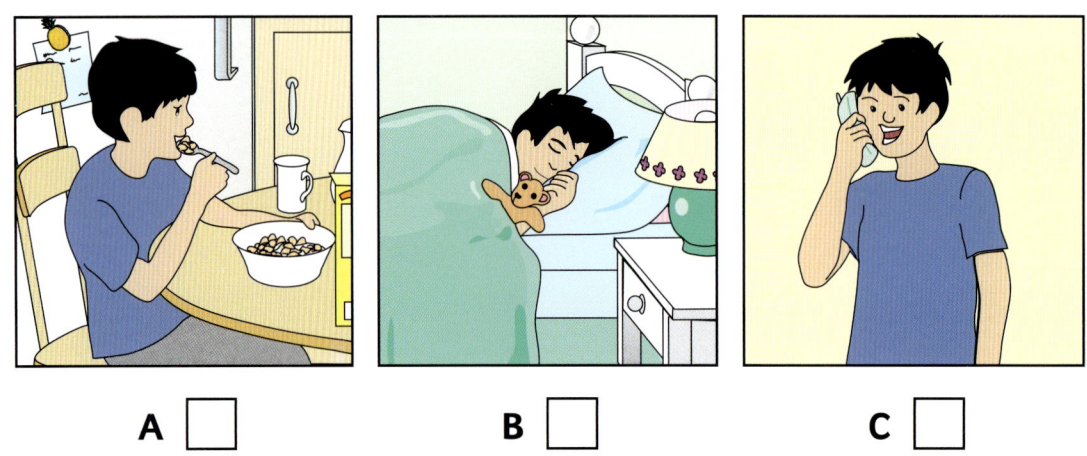

A ☐   B ☐   C ☐

3 Which animal is in the story today?

A ☐ B ☐ C ☐

4 Where is Anna's pen?

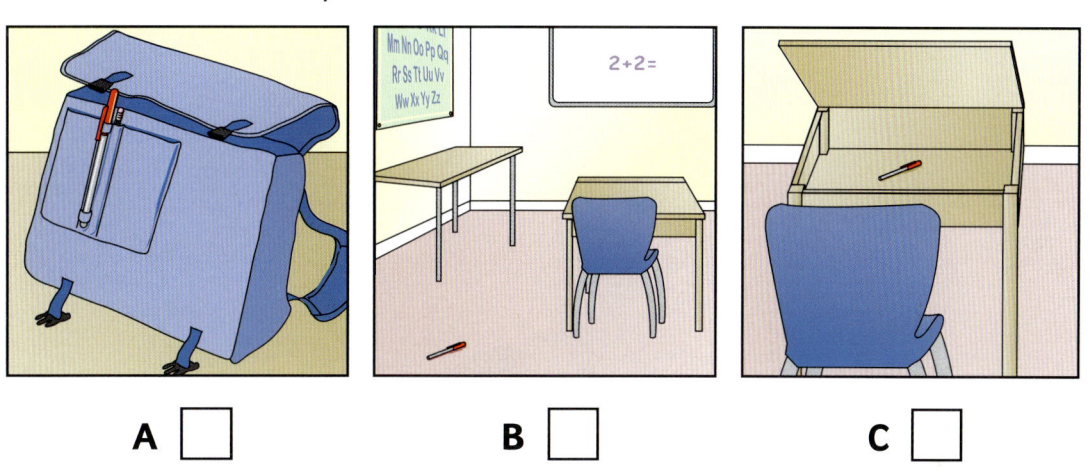

A ☐ B ☐ C ☐

5 Who's in the photo?

A ☐ B ☐ C ☐

Part 4

– 5 questions –

Listen and colour. There is one example.

Reading and Writing

Part 1

– 5 questions –

Look and read. Put a tick (✔) or a cross (✘) in the box.
There are two examples.

Examples

This is a camera.

This is a mouse.

Questions

1

This is the sun.

2

This is a jacket.

☐

3

This is a lizard.

☐

4

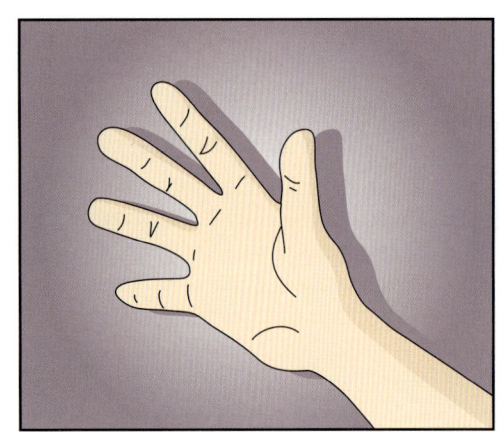

This is a head.

☐

5

This is a radio.

☐

Part 2
– 5 questions –

Look and read. Write yes or no.

Examples

The mother is reading.	yes
There are four cars on the beach.	no

Questions

1   A girl is riding a horse. ....

2   There are flowers on the mother's hat. ....

3   A small boy is swimming in the sea. ....

4   A big red shell is next to the robot. ....

5   The dog is on the mat. ....

Part 3
– 5 questions –

Look at the pictures. Look at the letters. Write the words.

Example

<u>b a s e b a l l</u>

Questions

1

_ _ _ _ _ _

2

_ _ _ _ _ _

3

_ _ _ _ _ _ _

4

_ _ _ _ _ _ _ _

5

_ _ _ _ _ _ _ _ _

Part 4

– 5 questions –

Read this. Choose a word from the box. Write the correct word next to numbers 1–5. There is one example.

A classroom

I am in a ....*school*........ . Children sit on small

(**1**)........................ and have lessons in me.

A (**2**)........................ stands in me and talks to the children.

She writes words on a big, white (**3**)........................ on the wall.

Children can play (**4**)........................ and watch the television.

They read (**5**)........................ , write stories and draw pictures in

me too.

What am I? I am a classroom.

Example			
school	juice	books	teacher
games	board	nose	chairs

Part 5

– 5 questions –

Look at the pictures and read the questions. Write one-word answers.

Examples

Where is the cake?   on the ....table........

How many babies are there?   ....two........

Questions

1   Which room are they in?   the ....

2   Who's opening the window?   the   ....

3   What's the baby doing?   ....

4   How many birds are there?   ....

5   What is the yellow bird eating?   the   ....

Blank Page

SCENE PICTURE

47

Blank Page

OBJECT CARDS

Test 1

Test 1

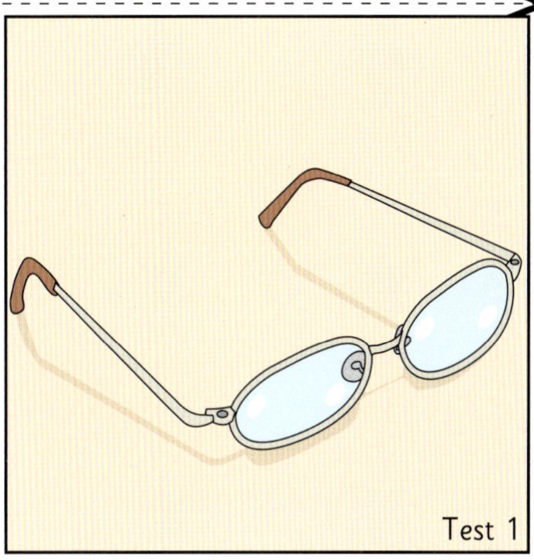

Test 1

Test 1

Test 1

Test 1

Test 1

Test 1

Blank Page

SCENE PICTURE

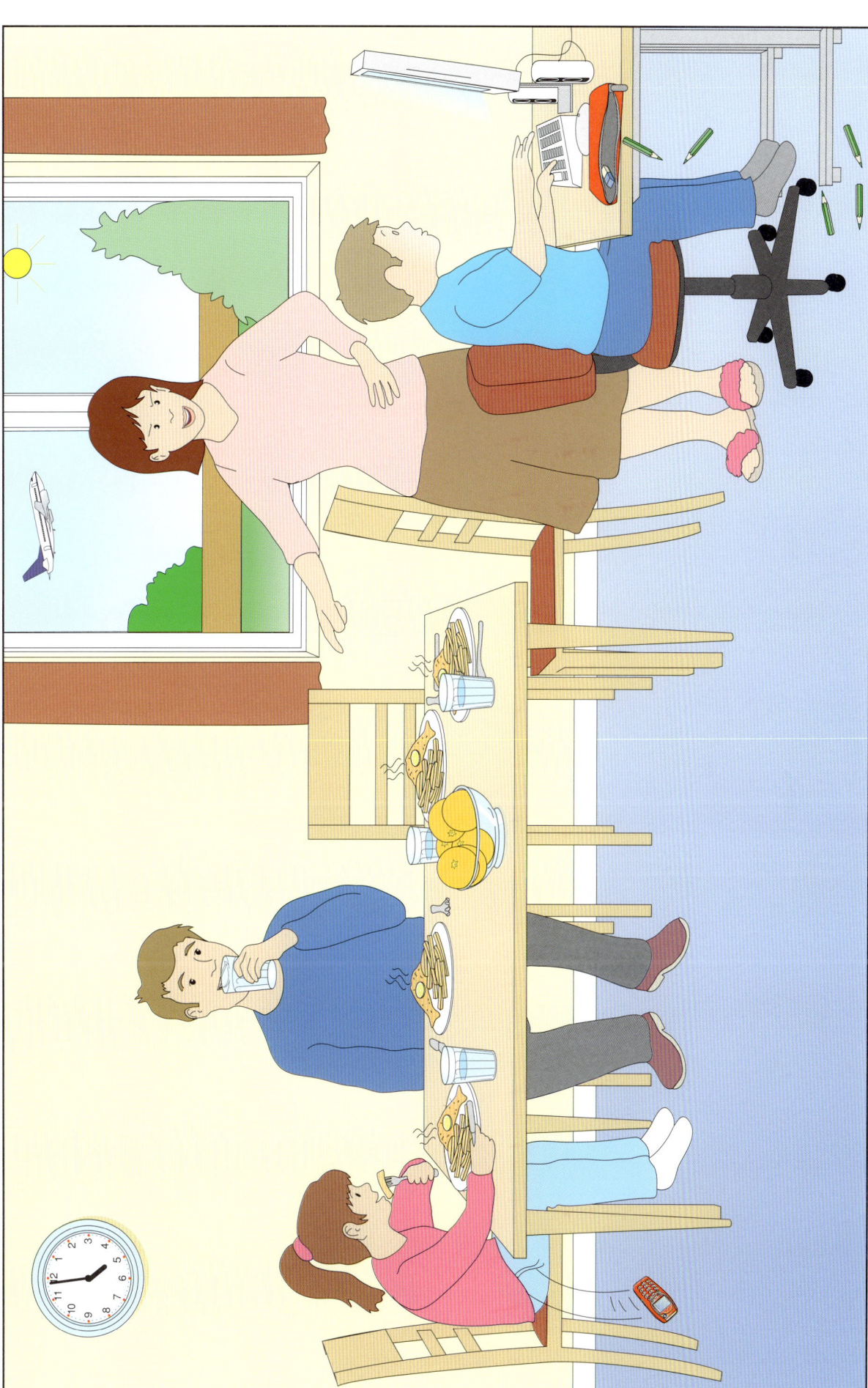

Blank Page

OBJECT CARDS

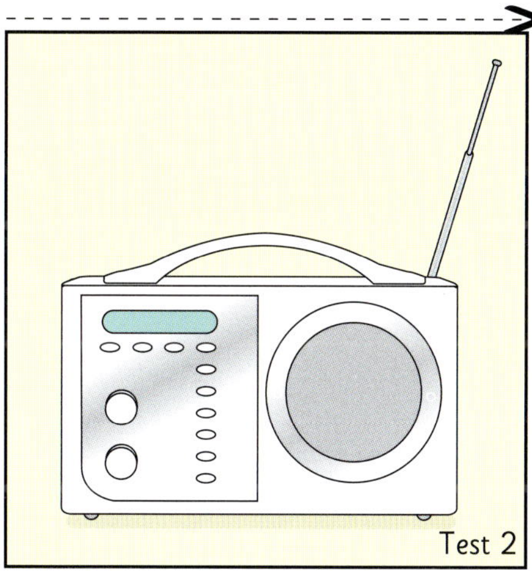

Test 2

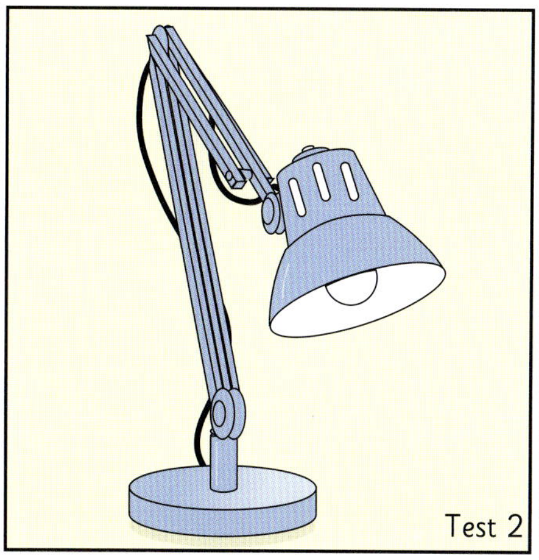

Test 2

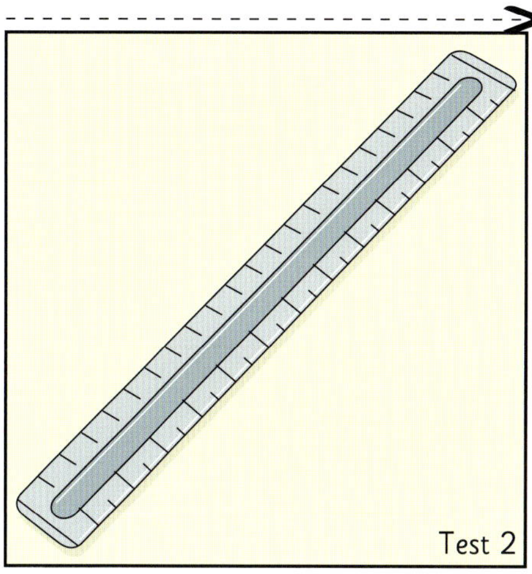

Test 2

Test 2

Test 2

Test 2

Test 2

Test 2

Blank Page

Speaking

SCENE PICTURE

Blank Page

OBJECT CARDS

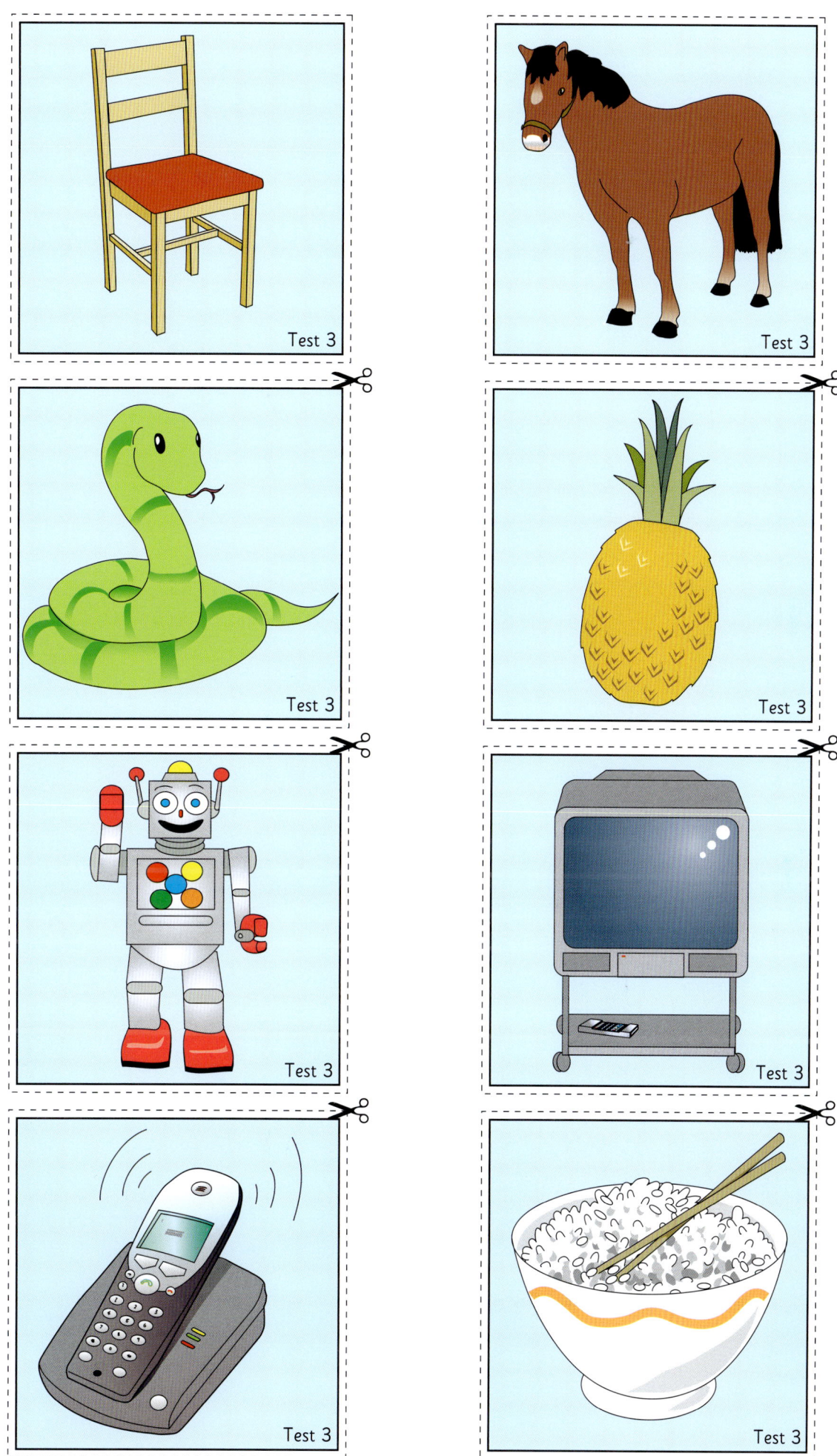